W9-AKC-730

LAP

DK READERS is a compelling program for beginning readers, designed in conjunction with leading literacy experts, including Dr. Linda Gambrell, Distinguished Professor of Education at Clemson University. Dr. Gambrell has served as President of the National Reading Conference, the College Reading Association, and the International Reading Association.

Beautiful illustrations and superb full-color photographs combine with engaging, easy-to-read stories to offer a fresh approach to each subject in the series. Each DK READER is guaranteed to capture a child's interest while developing his or her reading skills, general knowledge, and love of reading.

The five levels of DK READERS are aimed at different reading abilities, enabling you to choose the books that are exactly right for your child:

Pre-level 1: Learning to read
Level 1: Beginning to read
Level 2: Beginning to read alone
Level 3: Reading alone
Level 4: Proficient readers

DISCARD

The "normal" age at which a child begins to read can be anywhere from three to eight years old. Adult participation through the lower levels is very helpful for providing encouragement, discussing storylines, and sounding out unfamiliar words.

No matter which level you select, you can be sure that you are helping your child learn to read, then read to learn!

LONDON, NEW YORK, MUNICH,
MELBOURNE, and DELHI

Written by Fiona Lock

Series Editor Deborah Lock
U.S. Editor John Searcy
Project Art Editor Mary Sandberg
Production Editor Sean Daly
Production Erika Pepe
Jacket Designer Mary Sandberg

Reading Consultant
Linda Gambrell, Ph.D.

First American Edition, 2008
08 09 10 11 12 10 9 8 7 6 5 4 3 2 1
Published in the United States by DK Publishing
375 Hudson Street, New York, New York 10014

DK books are available at special discounts when purchased in bulk
for sales promotions, premiums, fund-raising, or educational use.
For details, contact:
DK Publishing Special Markets
375 Hudson Street
New York, New York 10014
SpecialSales@dk.com

A catalog record for this book
is available from the Library of Congress

ISBN: 978-0-7566-4093-4 (Paperback)
ISBN: 978-0-7566-4080-4 (Hardcover)

Color reproduction by Colourscan, Singapore
Printed and bound in China by L Rex Printing Co., Ltd.

The publisher would like to thank the following for their kind permission
to reproduce their photographs:
a=above; b=below; c=center; l=left; r=right; t=top
Alamy Images: Sally and Richard Greenhill 7tr; Picture Partners 4-5, 30-31;
Trevor Smith 14-15. **Corbis:** Paul Barton / Zefa 10-11; Heide Benser / Zefa
22-23; Alberto Biscaro 6-7; Jim Craigmyle 28-29; Richard Cummins 17tr;
Rick Gayle 13br, 13fbt; Paul Hardy 7bl; Dave G. Houser 24fbl; Richard
Hutchings 9tr; JLP / Sylvia Torres / Zefa 29tr; Moodboard 20-21; Touhig
Sion / Corbis Sygma 16-17; Ariel Skelley 21tr; Lee Snider / Photo Images
25tr; Tim Thompson 14tl. **DK Images:** The American Museum of Natural
History 18br, 18fbr, 18-19, 32bl; Robert L. Braun – modelmaker 17fbl; Jane
Bull 10fbr, 11br; Graham High at Centaur Studios – modelmaker 16fbr,
32tl; NASA 28br, 29fbr; NASA / Finley Holiday Films 29fbl; National
Railway Museum, New Delhi 24bc; Natural History Museum, London
16fbl, 17br, 17fbr, 19br; Stephen Oliver 9bl, 9fbl, 10fbl, 11bl, 30fbl; Royal
Tyrrell Museum of Palaeontology, Alberta, Canada 18c; Senckenberg,
Forschungsinstitut und Naturmuseum, Frankfurt. 19fbr; Washington Park
and Zoo Railway, Portland, Oregon 25bc; Jerry Young 21br. **Getty Images:**
Iconica / Blue Line Pictures 8-9; Stone / Richard Elliott 26-27. **NASA:**
26br, 27bl, 27br, 32clb. **Science Photo Library:** Indian Space Research
Organisation 26fbr; MSFC / NASA 26fbl; Starsem 27bc. **Shutterstock:**
Bianda Ahmad Hisham 14bl, 32cla; Alex Melnick 12-13.
Jacket images: *Front:* **Corbis:** Steve Kaufman bc; Tom & Dee Ann
McCarthy cla. **DK Images:** The American Museum of Natural History cl.
Shutterstock: Albert Campbell ftl.
All other images © Dorling Kindersley
For more information see: www.dkimages.com

Discover more at
www.dk.com

Contents

DK READERS

LEARNING TO READ

pre-level 1

Family Vacation

DK
DK Publishing

We went on vacation
for a week.

We packed our bags.

suitcase

We went on
an airplane.
We stayed in a hotel.

hotel

airplanes

swimming pool

On Monday, we went
to the beach.
We made
a big sandcastle.

sandcastle

beach

bucket

We splashed in the ocean
and then ate ice cream.

 ice cream

waves

theme park

On Tuesday, we went
to a theme park.
We went on some rides.

parade

We watched a parade.
There were lots of floats.

float

On Wednesday, we went to a dinosaur museum.

dinosaurs

teeth

We looked at
the skeletons.
Some were big and
some were small.

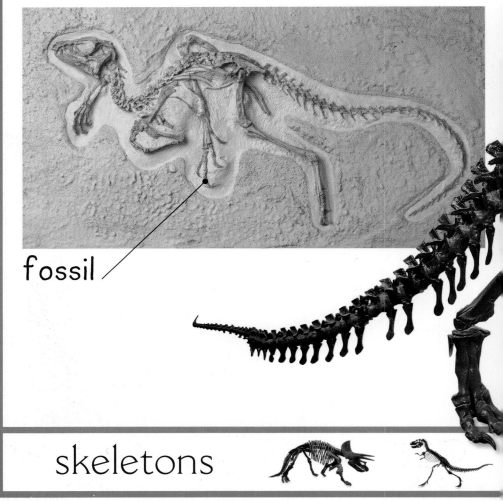

fossil

skeletons

skull

On Thursday,
we went for a walk.
We looked for bugs.

net

bugs

caterpillar

picnic basket

picnic

We had a picnic
in the park.

On Friday, we rode
on a train.
We went up
a steep mountain.

trains

track

On Saturday,
we looked at rockets
at a space center.

rockets

nose cone

We learned about the planets and the stars.

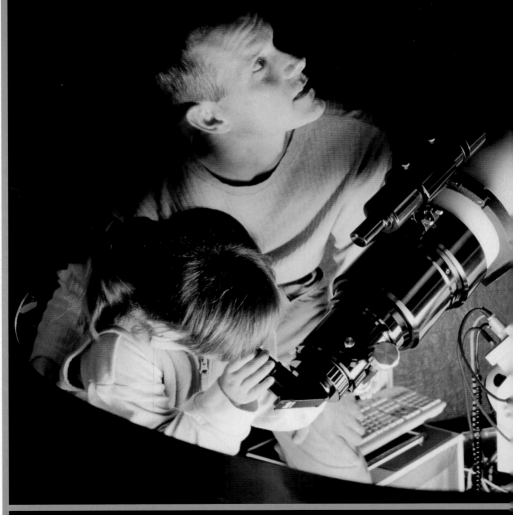

 planets

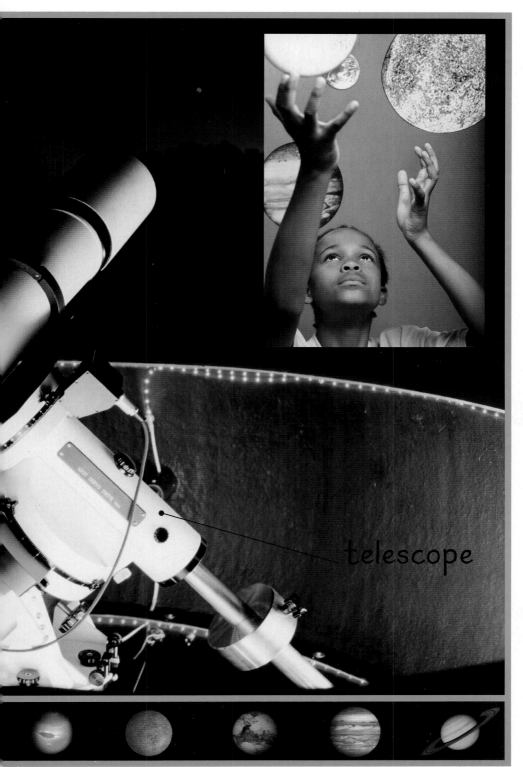

telescope

On Sunday,
we went home.
We looked at the photos
from our trip.

photo

What do you like